MOSAIC OF THE SUN

MARY HOXIE JONES

Mosaic
of the Sun

THE GOLDEN QUILL PRESS
Publishers

Francestown   New Hampshire

©THE GOLDEN QUILL PRESS 1975

811
J72

Library of Congress Catalog Card Number 75-22933

ISBN 0-8233-0233-4

Printed in the United States of America

To
"Poets Walk In"

Dear Poets, clothed with the sun
And sandalled with firelight,
By the wind of Parnassus
A trifle dishevelled . . .
How shall I tell you
The thanks in my heart
For this year's gifts,
For laughter, good talk,
Bread broken together
And the sharp, red wine of your poems?

–Elizabeth Gray Vining

ACKNOWLEDGMENTS

The author acknowledges the publication of some of these poems in *Friends Journal* and *The Golden Quill Anthology*; also her thanks to Elizabeth Gray Vining for permission to use her poem, *Dear Poets*, in the dedication.

CONTENTS

Gingko	13
Made for War	14
Marooned in Jerusalem	15
Christmas Should Be a Stillness	17
Genealogy	18
College Hair Styles	19
"The Kennedy Tomb Simple Design Outlined"	20
The Fawn	21
God and Satan	22
Keepsakes	24
Missing Connections at 30th Street Station	25
Violence	26
Akin to Cain	27
Christmas 1965	28
Vietnam	29
Asleep and Awake	30
Black-Eyed Susan	31
Christmas 1966	32
Hellish Communion	33
Noah	34
Birthday Candles	35
College Girl at the Railroad Station	36

Lost in Underbrush   37

What Time Is Now?   38

Gina Bachauer at the Piano   39

Christmas 1968   40

First Ice   41

Distance   42

Unforgivable Sin   44

Power Failure   45

Campus Styles   46

The Adventurer   47

The Rider   49

November   52

Citizen of Nirvana   53

Ashes No Longer   54

Confrontations   55

Holdup   61

Christmas 1971   62

Chase Hall — Haverford College   63

Magnolia   64

Not Even Icy Rock   65

Spanish Music for Lute and Guitar   66

Christmas Toys   68

The Chess Player   69

Grindelvald   70

Two Boys — 1873 and 1973   72

Birthday   74

The Idol   75

Spring in 1974   76

Top Stair and Bottom   77

Christmas 1974   78

San Damiano   79

What Is a Resurrection?   80

MOSAIC OF THE SUN

GINGKO

Golden against the sky
The gingko holds each leaf
Lace-patterned on the blue,
Instant of glory brief.
The swirling winds untie
To swim, like fish, a few
Gold coined leaves to lie
As though the ground were one
Mosaic of the sun.

MADE FOR WAR

Freud thought that sex
   Was our main drive,
A state complex
   On which we thrive;
Without, we're wrecks
   And half alive.

But now we see
   That war's the thing,
Sad normalcy
   To which we cling.
Man's hopelessly
   A violent being.

The hidden lust
   Is out of date.
Passion is just
   A normal trait;
Merely a must
   To propagate.

Man's made for war,
   And war for man.
He's relished gore
   Since time began.
He's nothing more
   Than orangutan!

(After reading *African Genesis*, by Robert Ardrey)

14

MAROONED IN JERUSALEM

I want to be ready,
I want to be ready
To walk in Jerusalem
Just like John.

You are too young
To walk into the New Jerusalem,
To have your tea
On the terraces of Heaven.

You, who worked for perfection,
Have now achieved it.
You, who gave beauty to others,
Now must receive it,
Too much beauty,
You will be surfeited with the sweet cakes
And ambrosia of Heaven.

On the close cut lawns
Of heavenly green
You can play an everlasting game
Rolling the croquet balls through golden wickets.
Who is your partner?
How are you faring among the angels?
What antiques can you find?
What bargains can you make
In the gift shops of Heaven?

It was not long ago
That you and I had tea together

On sunswept terraces.
Now I must drink the bitter tea of sorrow
Without you.
You are too young
To enter the New Jerusalem
Where I cannot follow.
Not even Heaven
Will have the olive trees
Which you and I remember.

CHRISTMAS SHOULD BE A STILLNESS

Christmas is now a frantic helter-skelter,
  A flurried grabbing, choosing bric-a-brac
For presents. And yet Mary still needs shelter,
  The donkey bears her burden on his back.

Radios blare of nights so still and holy,
  While Santa's bells keep up their constant jangle.
What has become of Mary, meek and lowly,
  Lost in the din, the glitter and the spangle?

Canned voices keep intoning "nights of silence",
  "So calm, so bright," "the Virgin and the Child."
While people in despair give way to violence,
  Harden their hearts, let bitterness run wild.

Christmas should be a stillness, not a worry,
  A gift of love, not any little thing
Bought on the run. A waiting, not a hurry.
  Christmas is glorious tidings angels bring.

GENEALOGY

How did I come by such progenitors,
I, the tag end of an illustrious line?
My veins now hold their blood. Its crimson pours
Through all my body, and their nerves define
My character. Great grandparents of mine

Levelled the forests of a wilderness,
And with their hands removed the stumps and stones,
Harrowed the ground, hoping the Lord would bless
Their labors, as He did. Their children's bones
Grew strong and straight, scions of Thomas Jones.

Thomas and Thankful, Lemuel and Wait,
Caleb and Peace. Such is my Family Tree,
Woodsmen and farmers, building their estate,
Passing their stubborness and vitality
Down through their sons and daughters and to me.

COLLEGE HAIR STYLES

You cannot imagine how weird
Is the boy with an Edward Lear beard.
   He works at his desk —
   His appearance grotesque —
Has Lear, with his beard, re-appeared?

Another, whose name is unknown,
Looks exactly like Solomon John,
   For dark on the chin
   Of this twin Peterkin,
Is a feebly, a soft growing down.

Like a terrier right out of Skye
With their locks drooping over the eye,
   The boys wear their hair,
   And through it they stare
At the world as it passes them by.

"THE KENNEDY TOMB
SIMPLE DESIGN OUTLINED"
(New York Times, November 17, 1964)

In all its bare simplicity
   The tomb embraces ash and bone.
A promise that his memory
   Will be enshrined in flame and stone,
To last in perpetuity.

The willow streams its dripping gold,
   And like an urn of polished brass
The beech tree gleams. November's old
   Decaying leaves lie on the grass,
And underneath the earth is cold.

And underneath, his ashes lie,
   His spirit gone, his ardor stilled.
The bright flame leaping to the sky
   Can never warm his passion killed.
The tomb, in its simplicity,
   With nothingness, with death is filled.

THE FAWN

One afternoon, against a wood,
   So lightly etched, so faintly drawn,
I scarcely could believe there stood
      A single fawn.

The trees were bare of leaves that day.
   In growing dusk the light was gone,
But like a silhouette in gray,
      I saw the fawn,

An instant only, as my train
   With gathered speed went thundering on.
Was it a dream? Yet on my brain
   Forever stands the deer, thus drawn
Against the trees, so faint, so plain,
      A sculptured fawn.

GOD AND SATAN

Where that of God
   And that of Sin
Leave off in me
   I can't begin

To understand.
   Why must I be
Torn by this fierce
   Dichotomy?

The Inner Christ,
   The Light Within,
The Seed, the Truth
   So seldom win.

The Devil spreads
   His trap. I fall
Into his hands.
   With Satan all

My better nature
   Ebbs away.
How strong his voice!
   I must obey

The Devil's urgings.
   Soon begin
My see-saw efforts
   Out of sin.

I teeter first
    One way, and find
My eye for goodness
    Has gone blind.

I teeter-totter
    Up and down,
While Satan conquers
    And I drown.

I teeter-totter
    Up again,
So goodness wins
    And God can reign.
But not for long.
The Devil's song
    Sings its refrain.

KEEPSAKES

All treasures which the heart has known
Are hidden, and are never shown,
Or lost in Time's oblivion.

But keepsakes of another age —
    The dolls, the spoons, embroideries,
A great aunt's thimble, or a page
    From diaries lost — she treasured these.

Her mother's pins, grandfather's seal,
    A little box, its contents lost,
These gave her comfort. She could feel
    Surrounded by the invisible host

Of family. She healed her pain,
Her sorrow with a broken cane,
With silk thread woven in a skein.

MISSING CONNECTIONS
AT 30TH STREET STATION

All efforts press to reach the moon.
   A doubtful pleasure it appears
   To me, who do not greet with cheers
The prospect of a flight there soon.

But countless thousands work away,
   And dollars by the millions pour
   To build Apollo. I deplore
The Pennsy's death-knell and decay.

I only want to ride to town —
   A dozen miles — without delay.
   I only want to get away
Without the Local breaking down.

To reach the moon is not my dream —
   A barren land in which to wake.
   A train without a frozen brake —
   A simple plea, is all I make
Of diesel or of steam.

VIOLENCE

The boy who set the bomb,
   Who threw the stone,
Who thrust the razored knife
   Into the bone,
   Lives in a world alone.

The blast, the broken glass,
   The frightened scream —
These are his one delight,
   Violence his dream.
   Blood in a scarlet stream

Quenches his thirst for love,
   His appetite is fed
By ruin and by storm,
   By a child left dead,
   Where rivers all run red.

AKIN TO CAIN

Fingers can do it, or a stone,
   Fingers can choke and close the breath.
Carefully aimed, or blindly thrown,
   A rock can crack the skull, a stone
   Is quick and hard and sure for death.

Our violence is as old as Cain
   Who flung his brother to the ground.
For reasons he could not explain
Hatred and anger seized on Cain,
   And Abel's blood streamed from his wound.

We curve our fingers on a stone
   Ready to hurl, we grasp a sword
Ready to plunge, for we have grown
Akin to Cain, with knife, with stone,
   With razor's slash and blood outpoured —
Murdered and murderer are one.

CHRISTMAS 1965

The shepherds' road is rough and hard
   Across deep furrows of a field,
Along steep paths where stones are sharp,
   On roads where dangers are concealed.
But shepherds with their dogs and sheep
Travelled to find the Child asleep.

The wisemen's road is long and hard
   Across the desert where the sand
Obliterates all tracks, where stark
   Lie treeless wastes of barren land.
But Magi came with myrrh and gold
To find the Child a star foretold.

My road is trackless too, and hard.
   I have no gift, I hear no song
Of angels, and I see no star.
   But if I press my way along
Persistent as the others were,
Let me too find the Child is there.

VIETNAM

When you strike the match
   You will see the flame
Creep along the thatch.
You will stand and watch.
  Soldier, who set the flame,
  Are you or I to blame?

For you have been brought
   Here only to kill.
For this the draft caught,
For this you are taught,
  Soldier, to learn one skill —
  Another's blood to spill.

But I uphold your torch,
   My taxes trained your hand.
What you now scorch,
The gun with which you search,
  Soldier, carries my brand,
  A curse from my land.

ASLEEP AND AWAKE

Night and day become separate
   As the cardinal whistles in joy
     From the tall tree.
No longer can dawn wait,
   For growing light will destroy
     Night's ebony.

I am brought from the depths of sleep,
   And wakened into the coming light
     By the cardinal.
Will it be thus I take the final leap,
   Brought into dawn from an endless night
     By Gabriel?

BLACK-EYED SUSAN

One black-eyed susan,
Strong in its rooting, high above the grass,
Brilliant in color, lifted by the wind,
Spoke without language.
This gay, wild flower gave
Assurance to us, seeing the body pass
As ashes to the ground; comfort to the mind;
Faith to see farther than this new formed grave
Where sun-burned grass and sun-baked clay
Swallowed these ashes, sucked down far away
Our friend to the mysterious element of ground.

The black-eyed susan grew
To bid her welcome at its fertile root,
To tell us gathered there around its foot
That immortality is simple, not profound.
We do not need to strain to understand.
We turned to go, thus comforted
To leave her ashes in this grave —
Our friend, too early dead —
When you
Snapped off the flower and held it in your hand.

CHRISTMAS 1966

Can your mother's arm
  Hold you safe in its curve,
Sheltered and warm?
  Or can her love serve

As shield from the rain,
  From the cold, from the bomb
With its burning and pain?
You had better remain
  Unborn in her womb.

For, Child though you are,
  We have said you must die
In spite of your star,
  Or the crib where you lie.
The wise men from far
  Are too late coming by.

(Set to music by Vally Weigl in December 1966 and copy-
righted and included in the Composers Facsimile Edition,
by Wally Weigl or the American Composers Alliance, New
York 1967.)

32

HELLISH COMMUNION

We do not give our bodies to be burned,
   Being too fond of life, loving the sound
Of spring now that the winter days have turned
   To longer sun and crocus through the ground.

The far off jungles ooze in the dark mud,
   Steaming with death, young soldiers clog the streams
Turning the water to a wine of blood —
   Hellish communion that will haunt our dreams.

Although we pray to have this cup removed,
   That we not burn nor drink, a tongue of flame
Unseen consumes us and the life we loved,
   Shrivels, destroys our souls. We look the same,
   Bodies alive, but soul-less in our shame.

NOAH

Who will be Noah and prepare an ark
   Three hundred cubits long of gopher wood?
   Gather the animals to breast a flood,
Prepare a voyage before the skies grow dark?
For rain is promised higher than the mark
   Of earlier tides, and where the mountains stood
   Their snows will redden in a sea of blood.
Noah! Build soon! Get ready to embark!
Add to the strange, exotic passenger list
   All weeds and grasses, every bush and tree.
     Noah! Build now! And add an extra room!
For when, if ever, a rainbow clears the mist,
   How shall a dove, sent forth upon this sea,
     Find even an olive branch still left in bloom?

BIRTHDAY CANDLES

The student said:
  "He lighted my candle."
The teacher said:
  "Man's spirit is the Lord's candle."
The sage said:
  "Curse not the darkness. It is better to light a candle."

Where the anniversary candles burned,
  The student was there.
  Though blind to the flickering flames,
His spirit was still radiant
  From the teacher's lighting.

The teacher was not there,
  But his voice, penetrating, arresting,
  Spoke again.
We were caught up with the spell
  Of his spirit, reminding us
That we are God's candle and His right hand.

We all became as wise as the sage,
Taking new hope from the candles
  And their flickering, fragile glowing.
For the light indeed does shine in the darkness,
And the darkness cannot put it out.

(The 50th anniversary, April 1917 - 1967, of the American
Friends Service Committee. The student is Howard H. Brin-
ton; the teacher, Rufus M. Jones, whose voice was heard on
a record, and the sage is Confucius.)

COLLEGE GIRL AT THE RAILROAD STATION

Periwinkle is the color of skies, of flowers, of seas.
But stepping across the railroad track,
Lifting each slender foot
In its patent-leather boot,
The girl, assured and blasé, walked with no look back.
Her mini-skirt, clinging, a doll's size,
Ended slightly below her hips.
Her periwinkle panty-hose climbed up her thighs,
Showing off to perfection bony, unattractive knees.

In my day, a fence
Divided station from station
Forbidding us to step over rails and ties.
We crossed, going sedately down steps, under
And up, in our long skirts and black silk hose.
Innocent school girls, gently aware, in wonder
Of the unknown, unmentioned, immense
Nebulous world of sex, or those
Strange beings involved with its consummation.

Now, with what ease the periwinkle nylons
Step across the once forbidden tracks and proclaim
The unmistakable readiness for Eden.

LOST IN UNDERBRUSH

She was afraid of the trees
Believing a wind could split their solid trunks
Or uproot them in a storm.
She was afraid of the trees
Which might fall on the house
And crush her to death.
She was afraid.

At her insistence
A saw cut through the firm wood,
Tossed great logs to the ground,
Hurled branches against new saplings,
Scattered slash among the ferns,
Left stumps to rot.
What is left of beauty in this wasteland?

She who was afraid
Of the blowing wind,
Of death from a falling tree
Clean and swift,
Was herself cut down
By disease creeping through her body,
Which she accepted apparently without fear.
She never saw the broken forest
Which we who loved her have inherited.

It was to the wind her ashes were given.
They are scattered among the ferns.
She is lost in the underbrush
Of her imagined fear.

WHAT TIME IS NOW?

What time is now?
The past and future crowd upon the here.
The leaf upon the bough
Is bud, full grown or sere
Falling in spiral flight.

When now is night
The dawn is near
Bringing tomorrow into sight.
When day is light
And yesterday has gone,
It still lives on
In minds remembering.

There is no spring
Except a moment's flight
Between the winter's cold
And summer's heat
Turning to autumn's gold.

The past and future meet
Where plow
Prepares the furrow
And reaper binds the grain.
None can explain
How the tomorrow
And the yesterday
Meet in the now.

GINA BACHAUER AT THE PIANO

The conductor, lifting his hand
Signals the opening beat.
Violinists draw their bows.
Watching the wand
Cellos and harps respond,
Viols and horns repeat
As the river of music flows.

Turning, he points his wand
And smiles as the lifted hand
Falls, like a dropping stone,
On the keyboard. Fingers move.
Their touch into chords create
Life from inanimate
White keys and tautened strings.
Fingers, the masters of
Music and trumpets blown
With mysterious summonings.

CHRISTMAS 1968

Bunchberry,
Bayberry,
Blueberry,
Blackberry,
Christmas is coming
And all will be merry.

Atom and H bomb,
Cobalt and napalm,
Sing carol and noel
And end with a psalm.

Famine and hunger,
Hatred and anger,
Christmas is coming,
With a Child in the manger.

Atom and H bomb,
Famine and anger,
O Child in the manger,
Can you hear as we quarrel,
Or the strains of our carol
Which ends with a psalm?

Bunchberry,
Bayberry,
Blueberry,
Blackberry,
Christmas is coming,
Be merry!   Be merry!

FIRST ICE

I walked along the shore
And saw that ice
Had formed the night before.
Stepping on crystal glass
I found it bore
One foot, one kick of heel.
I tried it twice,
Then heard the boom and crack.

Get back! Get back!
This surface is no more
Than gossamer and lace.
Get back! Get back!

I hugged the safer shore.
I am no pioneer.
When ice is frozen steel,
Safe for my feet to trace
Steps on a solid track
Undangerously to pass,
I shall come back.

DISTANCE

It is a long way
To Bethlehem,
To Tipperary,
To the moon.

It is a long way
To the Child in the manger,
To one's dream of home,
To the conquest of space.

But the black student
Goes an even longer journey
From his deep South
To the unknown North.
He crosses, but does not conquer,
The barriers of encounter.

And the man who takes his first step
Alone after a long illness,
Travels an incalculable distance.

It is a long way.
Christmas is over,
Tipperary is not there,
The moon keeps its accustomed phases,
And floats, still unattainable.

But the black student confronts his white classmate
And finds they ask the same questions of each other.
The lame man walks again

And takes long steps within himself
To discover his new direction.

UNFORGIVABLE SIN

Tasting the apple which grew
On the tree
Of knowledge of evil and good
Was forbidden, as Adam well knew.
But why, was the mystery.
And we
Who drown in the flood
Of all sin since Adam and Eve,
Could believe
We were washed of all guilt by the blood
Of Jesus on Calvary.

Was this just a mythical sign?
If so, what have we as reprieve?
Are the Bread and the Wine,
Christ's death on the Rood,
Merely tales to deceive?
Is my sin unforgivably mine?

POWER FAILURE

There is no power.
Everything has come to a standstill.
A tree, blown by the wind,
Has come down on the wires
And they have snapped.
No light, no train,
Just a broken cable
And a rotten tree
Sprawled on the track.

But men are already at work
Cutting up the branches,
Climbing the pole for repairs.
They know the intricate mechanisms
For restoration.

I have no axe for cutting,
No ladder, no new cable,
No workmen to call in.
When the cataclysm breaks my connections
So that my inner light flickers
And all power fails,
It is for me to remove the debris
And start the process
Of restoration.

CAMPUS STYLES

The students pass
  Outside my window
Into class.
Hair long, uncombed,
  And beards untrimmed,
Their jackets torn,
  Their legs, long limbed
In dirty jeans.
Oh, unwashed Seekers
  After Truth,
So arrogant,
  So sure in youth,
  So unattractive and uncouth
In sandals or in ragged sneakers,
Beneath this hair
  And sloppy dress,
No doubt there dwells
  A rare noblesse,
Each bosom swells
  With tenderness.

Aesthetically
  You are a mess.

THE ADVENTURER

You have set forth
On so many adventures,
Walking the miles
Which lead to all places.
As you walked you have observed
The change of seasons,
The growth of flowers and trees,
The growth of children,
Of men and women,
The creation of cities,
The building of community.

You have set forth
On so many adventures
Which have not used footsteps,
Nor clocked mileage.
You have visited
The unknown depths and heights
Of the mind's ocean,
Of the heart's mountain.
You have discovered
Reasons for sorrow,
Roots for joy.
You have travelled the distance
From one person to another,
Listened and spoken,
Knowing the time for each
Out of your own wisdom.

You have set forth
On so many adventures,
Each one, on foot or in spirit,
Bringing you stature,
Tallness which cannot be measured.

THE RIDER
(W.R.J. 1902 - 1970)

Charlbury 1908
He was the engine,
And the engineer,
The brakeman
And the locomotive's bell.
He chugged forward,
And shunted backward,
On invisible tracks,
Clanging the bell
Cast out of his imagination.

Dirigo Road 1927
The Model T was real and black.
He drove it like a mad man
On an obstacle race.
It shivered and rattled on the road,
He shouted in the dark,
To me beside him, listening,
To the unhearing woods around us.
He swerved away from ditches,
He crashed around curves,
He bumped over the ledges.
"In dulce jubilo!"
He was in love.

China Lake 1952
It was his boat.
As the sheet filled
And we sailed into the wind

49

He put my hand on the tiller.
As we talked quietly
A sudden gust took the sail.
We were over in a second,
Floundering in the water.
We climbed aboard again,
But he did the steering.
"Ready about, hard lee."
With the turning, he and the tiller
Slid into the rough water.
His boat and I sped on.
The ropes, held taut in my fingers,
Somehow obeyed me,
They let down the sails.
We met in the shallow water
Where he swam with the rudder.
I returned his boat to him.

Rockland Ferry 1970
Now he is on the ship which runs a daily
    course
Across Penobscot Bay,
Where he knew every depth and shoal
From his chart's soundings.
The imaginary engineer,
The Model T driver,
The sailor and swimmer
Are distilled and refined
Into wholeness.
His ashes fall into the blue water
Floating and rising with the waves,
And the bell which he used to ring

Tolls for the new sailor
On a new sea.

NOVEMBER

Slow circling leaf
That spirals down
From twig to grass,
From grass to me.
Red leaf and gold,
Yellow and brown,
Copper and brass,
With you I hold
The flaming tree.
With you I see
The gray new fold
Of buds, the crown
Of fruit to be.

CITIZEN OF NIRVANA
(Between Boston and Philadelphia)

Floating above clouds
Which are a tranquil sea,
Then shift into arctic snow fields,
And eventually become a heap of egret feathers,
I find it hard to remember
That underneath this opaque curtain
Lie turmoil and uncertainty,
People who tilt at windmills,
Who live in slums and ghettoes,
Who breathe in air, already polluted,
And breathe out their smog of frustration.

The earth is hidden.
It presents no threat, no challenge,
No Babel of mixed voices.
Bearded men with their testimonies,
The Pentagon, with its perfected science of destruction,
Vietnam, with its hideous crusade,
Are non-existent.

I balance
In this blue, sunlit dimension of heaven
Gratefully a citizen of Nirvana.
The two little boys across the aisle,
Unable to be part of such an experience,
Ask the stewardess, in their urgency,
For another Coke.

ASHES NO LONGER

Now in the Bay
Spring tides return
And float the ice to sea.
How can I learn
That you have gone away
And cannot be
Summoned at will? The gray
Ice crumbles in the warm
Spring sun. Your ashes lay
Prisoned by winter and its freezing storm.

Now, on your birthday, they
Lift in the open water
Ashes no longer.
You are swimming free.

CONFRONTATIONS

(At Philadelphia Yearly Meeting of
the Religious Society of Friends.)

I.

Christianity or Flower Children?   1968
Whether or not we are Christians
Is today's perplexing question.
The angry young men say: NO,
Christians are phonies and queer,
Lying and insincere,
Establishment symbols who follow
A Master long dead. They swallow
Christ's teachings long proved to be hollow,
And better forgotten.

The angry young men say: NO,
Jesus died long ago,
And what did anyone gain
From His meekness, His pain,
Or His rising again —
God's only Begotten?

But the angry young men who wear
Their beads and their beards and long hair
Resemble the Man they scorn.
While they call Him a knave, a fool
Who started a cult outworn,
And taunt Him with ridicule,
They follow Him none the less
In looks and manner of dress.
And still more ironic and odd,

The angry young men who say: NO
Consider themselves to be God.

II.

Racism 1969

The talk goes on
Like rivers in their flood,
Sticks, branches from the mud
Uprooted, swirl, while Black
Confronts the crowded room
Filled with White faces strained
Against this rush
Of words in the attack.

Outside, magnolias bloom,
And spring's resurgent push
Brings the familiar resurrection back.

The Whites, called hypocrites, are drowned
By all these words, spat from a bitter tongue.
Damned by the Black,
And by the Young
Misunderstood.

Where is an Ararat of higher ground
To give us mooring from this flood of sound?

III.

Reparations 1969

If I pay you what you demand
Will this repair
Past sins,
Past grievances my people brought
Unthinking? Where begins
New justice? For we both are caught
In systems both unfair
And wrong. And yet we glare
With this demand,
And meet each other with clenched fist,
Weapons concealed
Ready to give the knife a twist
In cringing flesh. Who will yield?
This method will not get us anywhere.
Will you or I be healed
Taking my dollars?
Rather, take my hand.

IV.

The Establishment 1970
Our voices rise
In strident words.
The Spirit dies.
We are like birds
Perching in trees to shout
Our territorial rights.

What is this all about?
Aid to the Blacks —
Disparagement of Whites —
The worshipping of bricks —
Instead of pouring love
We pour cement
Which hardens all the cracks.
What can this argument
In all its phases prove?
It only stiffens backs
And fosters more dissent.

Let silence come.
Open the doors and see
The star magnolia tree
Break into bloom!

V.

"Frozen Christian" 1971

Those who advocate
And search for methods to create
Some new approaches to a social change,
Feel heavily upon them the dead weight
Of my short comings. They enumerate
My faults, my failures, but they fail to see
The grimness of their faces. It is strange
They cannot smile. They cannot be
At all objective,
But with harsh invective
Of word and tone insist that I am wrong,
And they are right.
No one shall railroad them, so free
To push the world along.

Smile, rigid changer, smile, and show less hate.
"Bloom, frozen Christian, bloom." Initiate
Within ourselves a change.
Our inner darkness must give way to light.

VI.

Answer to the Black Manifesto 1971

The Meeting gathered, and the Lord
Was like a cover, like a cloud
Spread over all.
No one allowed
His fear to show by word
Or sound. No call
Was made to move our uninvited guests
From seats usurped. All their protests
Were heard.

But then the Lord
Took over and all heads were bowed,
And thus let fall
Our rage and fear.
Answers before unclear
Were sure, although
They must be NO.

The Lord was here.

HOLDUP

Come on, woman, don't cling
    To your bag.
    I shall drag
It away. Your money's the thing
I shall get, for I've got
To have dough for a shot.

Come, woman, let go!
    Yes I know
    I am Black,
And a knife in your back
Makes your fingers go slack.

My knife is my friend.
It gets me the dough
    In the end.
Come on, let it go!
    My knife
    Is my life,
As a Black ought to know.

CHRISTMAS 1971

Motor inns
Have no vacancies.
Highways
Have a minimum
Speed limit
Impossible for a donkey.

What happens to weary travellers
When there are no rest areas,
And, unlike a stable,
The garage has no manger?

Suddenly we are confronted by a Star
And the voices of angels singing.
The Time has come
And there is no room.
No room,
Unless we allow
The Birth to take place
Within ourselves.

The ivy turns red
   Against the gray stone,
Leaves fall on the path
   His footsteps have known.
   The oak leaves are blown
And drift brown and dead.

I look at the gray
   Of the stone and the red
Of the ivy he loved
   And the leaves. He is dead.
   Is all that he said
In the wind tossed away?

Boys open the door
   Through the ivy and stone
Where he entered to teach,
   But like the leaves blown,
   The teacher is gone,
He comes here no more.
   Can he still light their candles
From his distant shore,
   Remembering ivy,
   Remembering stone?

MAGNOLIA

Cut off a magnolia twig,
Put it in water in a warm room,
The tight buds will swell,
Grow big,
Crack the velvety shell,
And bloom.

Flowers for the new year, when spring
Is still light years away,
Lift up the wintry heart
To sing.
April will start
Today.

NOT EVEN ICY ROCK

Three robins listening
   Are running on frozen grass,
   And as I pass
I know that spring
Has come again, although
   The ground
   Is bound
With ice. That snow
   In heaps still lies
In shadowed corners, where
   No sun can fall
   At all.

A crocus pries
   Its petals to the air.
   Not even icy rock
   Can block
This urgent push of bloom
Whose time has come —
   This prompt returning flock
Of robins, and the call
Clear from the wintry skies,
   Of cardinal.

SPANISH MUSIC FOR LUTE AND GUITAR

Through leaded panes
Lead gray beech trees spread
Against a cloudy, leaden sky.
Bare branches are etched against clouds,
Gray on gray,
A charcoal drawing.
Through leaded panes
Sunset flames. The trees stand
Against a golden sky.

The Renaissance Boy —
The Botticelli Angel — in a tailored suit,
Plucks on his lute
Playing angelic music.

Silhouetted through another window
Is a green pine tree,
Its feathery branches
Waving in the wind
Against a blue sky.

And the Renaissance Boy,
The Botticelli Angel,
Plucks out music
On his guitar.

The sunset fades;
Dusk closes in.
Chandelier lights
Turn into golden balls

Reflected on gray beeches,
And on green pine.
This is now a timeless season
Of light and music.

The Renaissance Boy,
The Botticelli Angel
Plays on.

CHRISTMAS TOYS

Christmas as a time of wonder
We thought we had outgrown.
It could never come again
Now that we are adults,
No longer children.
Suddenly we were children
Looking with wonder
To see the doll, the train
We each had known.

Here like a dream, our childhood
Had come back.
Your train that rushed along a track
Through molded valleys and steep hills;
My doll that wore a white embroidered dress,
With its old-fashioned frills
Brought us, that instant
Into timelessness.

Christmas forever,
Never
To be outgrown.
A star-lit wonder
All our own.

(Christmas toy exhibit at Brandywine River Museum,
Chadds Ford, Pa.)

THE CHESS PLAYER
(R.J. died December 22, 1972)

When the table was ready,
He set up the board,
White squares and black squares,
Dusted and steady.

He carefully poured
The ivory chess men
Out of their case,
Set them in pairs —
Castle and bishop,
A pawn and a queen —
Each in its place.
A moment to clean
The bowl of his pipe
And to fill it again.
Then the game can begin.

Begin with his move
Cautious and sure,
Certain to prove
His skill can endure.

Begin with his move,
And keep on with the game
Till the eighth row is made,
And the pawn is withdrawn,
And transformed in his name.
For he died as he played.

GRINDELVALD
1908 - 1973
(For J.W.R.)

Grindelvald has covered our conscious existence
With the double rainbow we saw as children.
Taken out of bed,
Held in our parents' arms,
We saw this iris ribbon of color.

Your mother, my father
Hoped we would remember.
Remember!
We have never forgotten.
Of the gifts they gave us,
Love, security, widening of horizons,
The rainbow, that instant's glory,
Is another which lasts forever.

In these intervening years,
No longer children,
We have climbed the paths
Of many mountains,
Crossed moors and fields
Green with shimmering barley,
Picked gentians, heather, primroses,
Touched the blue columbine,
Searched for the lady slipper,
Seen sunsets and sunrises,
Moonlight on glaciers,
Shared laughter and sorrow.

We are old women now,
Separated by an ocean,
Plagued with unanswerable questions,
But sixty-five years after Grindelvald
We climbed the steep paths,
Leaving behind all burdens
Except the bread and cheese in our rucksacs.

The rainbow, supposedly unattainable,
Has left its pot of gold deep in our hearts,
Invisible, intangible,
But real in its existence,
Still beautiful,
Still remembered.

TWO BOYS — 1873 and 1973

One boy, a hundred years ago,
Weeding potatoes, stopped in the row
And said to his father,
Leaning on his hoe:
"I want to go away to school,
Go away from here,
From this farm and field I know;
I want education, to get the tool
To make my life count.
Without it I am a mere
Nothing. I want to amount
To something. I want to go away."

Another boy, today,
Rootless, footloose,
A college drop-out,
Who has a trace
Of the same family strain,
The same pioneer blood in his vein,
Said: "I am not going back to school.
After a year I know
It has nothing for me.
It's very plain
That what I want to be
Does not come from school.
I don't want to learn.
I want to turn
Furrows with a plough,
Grow tall corn, make bread,
Milk a cow.

"Life looks good from this perspective.
I want to get my feet on the ground,
And learn to live.
Perhaps then the lost can be found,
And I can make a start.
I don't want more things in my head,
But in my heart."

BIRTHDAY

(January 25, 1863 - January 25, 1974)

As each returning birthday brings again
Another cold and snowy night to mark the time,
Only a few remember and rejoice
That long ago a mother held her son,
New born and crying.
And, when night was done,
Aunt Peace, with her prophetic voice,
Spoke of your travels to a foreign clime
To preach the Gospel, bringing truth and light.
Your mother's pain
Was eased at last.

Over a hundred years have passed
Since then, and you are lying
Beneath the snow and rain,
The prophecy fulfilled,
Your strong voice stilled.

But snow drops come
Through frozen ground along the way
This winter day
That marks your birth.
Only a few remember. Though the tomb
May hold your body in the earth,
Your buoyant spirit breaks in bloom.

THE IDOL

A woman's figure carved from wood,
Her oriental features kissed
Almost to nothingness, and stroked
By restless lips and fingers, smooth and flat,
Has always stood,
Strange idol, as a guardian of your room.
Now she has come
As guardian of mine.

What desperate souls invoked
Her mercy, or what hands held up a list
Of prayers for her unseeing eyes
To wonder at?
She, thought to be all wise,
Would give a sign.

What do I now expect
Of her, whom reverently I dust,
And touch with love, remembering
She was your idol? Can your intellect,
Your mystical awareness and your trust
Come back through her? Can this wood goddess
    bring
To me
Some inkling of remote Divinity?

SPRING IN 1974

As the leaves unfold,
And the dogwood is a white cloud,
The azaleas' flame brings lifting to the heart
To dance, like Wordsworth and his daffodils.
Never has grass been more green,
Nor dandelions more gold,
The cardinal is loud
In his whistling joy. I am a part
Of what this spring fulfills,
A part of this clean
Beautiful world.

      Yet I am bowed
With the sorrows and frailness of the old,
Their uncertain memories as they wait
For the peace that does not come. The bold,
Sordid manipulations of Watergate,
Unmoral in its power-seeking, obscene
In its twisting, serpent-like hold
Which strangles my heart.

TOP STAIR AND BOTTOM
(H.J.C. died October 7, 1974)

Seven years old:
      Run, leap down the stair,
      Small boy, to your game,
      To your book, to a friend —
      You, standing there
      At the top of the stair,
      We see you descend
      To the life that will claim
      The flame
      Of your mind,
      A pattern designed
      To bring pleasure and fame.

Almost ninety-one years old:
      We see you descend
      From the top of the stair.
      Go slowly, with care
      As you carry her tray.
      But you hurried away
      And found a new friend,
      For Death waited there
      At the end
      Of the stair.

CHRISTMAS 1974

The Wise Men came,
Led by a star's flame,
And brought their gold,
Their frankincense
And myrrh.
How could the Baby hold,
In tiny hand
Such gifts, or understand
The reverence,
The stir
The Wise Men brought?

And we, long taught
This tale of star
Bringing men from afar
To Bethlehem,
What gifts have we
To bring?

The myrrh of death,
The gold of greed,
The incense of pollution
We lift for Him to see.
Yet, to our sickened breath,
The poisoned stem
Of bitter need,
And our own destitution,
The Angels sing.

SAN DAMIANO

Walking between
A grove of olives and a wall
Behind which cypresses, a darker green
Than silvery olive leaf,
Stand tall,
We climb the sloping path and see
St. Francis walk ahead —
At least for one brief
Moment it is he.

And as we climb
No word is said
By you or me,
Too deep have our emotions been.

Perhaps another time
We can discover the right word
Which could describe
How each of us had seen
The very presence of our Lord.

WHAT IS A RESURRECTION?

Help Thou my unbelief,
Who cannot see the wound
Nor touch the side
Like Thomas. But I see the ground
Break open for the leaf
And bloom of daffodil;
Give way to let the worm
Do its accustomed ploughing.

Am I not satisfied
To see the wide
Melodious skein of geese
Move northward as they fill
The sky?

What is it to die?
To cease
From growing?
Perhaps it is a winter, when the stone
Is sealed until a spring,
And I become new grown,
Though old in root.
The stone, against my foot,
Can fall asunder,
And I, in wonder,
Achieve new blossoming.

811   J72   493-76

Jones
MOSAIC OF T

DATE DUE

AG6 '76	

811   J72

Jones
MOSAIC OF THE SUN   493-76

DATE DUE

AG6 76   BORROWER'S NAME